Engineers Work With Pulleys

Branca Tani

Rosen REAL READERS

Rosen Classroom™
New York

Engineers make tools. Tools make work easier. A pulley is a tool that lifts heavy things.

Pulleys help get water from a **well**. They help lift a heavy bucket of water.

Pulleys look like a wheel. A rope goes around the wheel. As the rope is pulled, the wheel moves. The wheel and rope work together to lift the **load**.

Many people use pulleys. Climbers use pulleys. If they fall, the rope of the pulley will hold them.

Engineers use pulleys to lift and move large rocks. **Simple machines** work with bigger machines to get work done.

This **rescue** helicopter has a pulley. The pulley lowers a worker. He helps someone in trouble. The pulley lifts them back up.

Pulleys are used on boats. Pulleys on boats are called blocks. This kind of pulley is usually made of wood. It uses a rope to lift the load.

Engineers make special drawings. They help them do their job. They draw all the parts of the machine they want to build.

Engineers visit the sites where pulleys and other machines are used. They make sure the machines work well. Engineers can help fix a pulley that is not working well.

Engineers make pulleys that people use for fun things, too. A pulley helps this girl zip down the zipline safely. Can you think of any other kinds of pulleys?

Glossary

load The weight of something that must be carried or moved.

rescue To save something or someone.

simple machine Any basic machine used to apply force, such as a wedge, lever, or pulley.

well A hole in the ground that provides clean underground water.